Other Books by T.K. Galarneau

The Arrangement
A Cowboy Tradition: Poems From the Heart
Dusty Rose, Gus & Me
Meadow Muffins in the Trail: Dodging Life's Little Disasters
Ruminations of an Old Woman

T.K. GALARNEAU

Sure Ain't Like IT USED TO BE

The Vanishing West

GusGus Press • Fairfield, California

978-1-960373-28-1 paperback

Cover Design
by
Sapling Studio

GusGus Press
a division of
Bedazzled Ink Publishing Company
Fairfield, California
http://www.bedazzledink.com

An Early Start

The sun's not yet up, but it's time to go
My pony is saddled, she's waitin' on me
There's cattle to find and bring to the pens
We'll doctor and brand, sort and load up
Some go to market, some go to pasture
This way of life is as old as the west.

From north to south and west to east
From the Pacific to the Mississippi
Buckaroos, vaqueros and cowboys
A man and his pony working the land
The names are some different but from
Sun up to sun set the work is the same.

Our western lifestyle is rich in tradition
From Spanish vaquero with garrocha in hand
Working their herds on Andalusia's plain
Man and nature in close harmony
The conquistadors to the new world came
They brought their cattle; a lifestyle was born.

The new world was rough; things had to change
Old ways were fixed from garrocha to lariat
The new vaquero changed with the times
Shotguns and batwings, armitas, and chinks
Slick or swell, center fire or full double rigged
Texas skirts, California skirts, tapaderos or oxbows

From California to Montana and Nevada to Texas
Huge ranches were built to work the herds
Texas punchers tied hard and fast
California vaqueros let their rope slide
Sixty foot rawhide or thirty foot hemp
Their job was to rope 'em and bring 'em in

It don't much matter where ya might work
It really don't matter the method ya use
A cowboy's a cowboy, his job hasn't changed
He's still workin' cattle out on the range
Ya can sure as heck bet year in and year out
He's startin' out early while it's still dark.

There must be a place where animals can live
Without interference from human concerns
So when the end comes, I pray constantly

No Respect

There was a time not too long ago
Man and nature lived in harmony

The Creator laid out His master plan
With animals and man close at hand

A family with each other prayed
On Mother Earth they did reside

The circle of life went on and on
All life that could be relied upon

For generations we lived this way
But things are different this day and age

Man has destroyed so many things
His lust and greed he needed to assuage

He raped the land and took all he could
Gold and silver, oil and coal, these things he stole

He killed the animals with no remorse
The buffalo and grizzly were on the brink

Coyote and wolves were vermin to die
Even prairie dogs had no place in this world

He built up the cities and tore up the plains
The wild places were on the endangered list

Eagles and peregrines were dying out too
The chemicals and pesticides were doing their job

Mother Earth Herself was terminally ill
The air and water were polluted and foul

Only until man was in danger of dying himself
Did right thinking people get hold of themselves

They cleaned up their mess and the distress was less
But the damage was done, Mother Earth bore the scars

Big business have us all by the throat
The powers that be even dance to their tune

Oil spills and pipelines scar our lands
Still the white man has no respect

When Mother Earth could give no more
The Creator took hold and punished us all

He called Mother Nature to bring down her wrath
Fires and floods have ravaged all in Her path

Winds fanned the flames and destroyed everything
In all Her fury Mother Nature ravaged Mother Earth

The good and the bad have to share this pain
Few were spared from the storm's bloody stain

Those who are left to rebuild and replace
Must remove the scars on Mother Earth's face

In the midst of all this devastation and sorrow
Love and compassion brings hope for tomorrow

People have come together to ease the pain
Of those who have lost without thinking of gain

A shoulder to lean on, an embrace to show care
These simple gestures give strength to repair

No doubt man will rebuild his cities much bigger
They should be careful if they don't figure

Out his is a cautionary tale of the result of greed
When people take more than they need

Without a thought for there is a buffer
When Mother Earth is made to suffer

When we pay no respect to this land
In the end there will be no place to stand

In some future time Creator and Mother Earth
May forgive man's transgressions and move on

But how many chances do you think
They will give us because in a blink

All that we know, if we fail to show
Love and respect for all that is given

When the last bridge has been crossed
And all has been lost; what's the final cost

Ask Mother Earth, only she can foretell
If man has struck his own death knell.

Riding the Circle

The sun's just come up; it's clearin' the rise.
The coffee is hot, it's ready in time
To clear my head and warm up my gut
I've got to get movin' there's no time to waste.

Down in the pens the horses are waitin'
I've got my string picked and ready to ride.
The circle is wide and the country is rough
My ponies are ready, I'll tell ya they're tough

Day in and day out, through blizzards and storms
The weather won't stop me from cuttin' the circle
I'll be lookin' for mavericks that's been lost;
I'm sure to find them no matter the cost.

Those critters is smart and some just plain mean
They'll try me and my horse to any extreme
Arroyos and streams, bogs and mesquite
Cactus will tear up my chinks and pull at my shirt.

The dust and grit gets in my eyes and teeth
My mouth is as dry as cotton in July
My pony's hide shines in the sun
Sweat from my body soaked my shirt.

Rain falls in sheets and slams in my face
My pony is drenched clear through his hide
The trail's so muddy we slip and slide
But ol Buck keeps his feet as we ride.

Thunder booms and lightning flashes
Some of them cows with horns so long
That with each lightning strike
Get that eerie glow of St. Elmo's fire.

The circle I ride reaches far and wide
A section so vast anything can hide
Ya do your best to make sure ya find
The remnants of those ya left behind

Ev'r now and again ya know there'll be
A shelly cow and come leppy calves.
Ya bring 'em in slow so they can rest
You'll carry a calf so he won't be lost

From dawn 'til dark the circle I ride
I get back to camp come ev'nin' time
My pony's bone tired and so am I
We'll do 'er again come mornin' time.

Sure Ain't Like It Used to Be

Things sure have changed since '51,
The day that on June 15th.
There weren't no Internet,
Hell, we lived without TV.

Sure ain't like it used to be.

We did the chores by hand, you see.
We took pride in what we did.
"That's ain't in my job description."
Came around in two thousand three.

Sure ain't like it used to be.

Dogs and ponies helped us out.
Had no such things as ATV's.
We herded cattle slow and easy.
'Cause every pound was valuable.

Sure ain't like it used to be.

The towns were small.
Your neighbors were close.
They'd lend a hand
If ever the need arose.

Sure ain't like it used to be.

Sunday rolled 'round; we all went to church.
We chatted awhile 'bout the price of beef
'Til country fried chicken called us away
Everyone gave thanks for all that we had.

Sure ain't like it used to be.

If ever there came a time,
When you gave your word,
You n'er took it back,
No matter what came 'round.

Sure ain't like it used to be.

There was something sacred 'bout
Pride, honesty, and integrity.
Meant what they meant
They weren't just words ya said.

Sure ain't like it used to be.

The Rancher's Tan

If ya travel down to Venice beach,
I'll tell ya what you'll find.
A lot's of lusty fine young men
Their muscles well-defined.
And coverin' them pectorals
All the way from head to toe
Is a shiny bronze-colored hide.

I guess ya'd have to work
Real hard on that there physique
To get the way they are
They lather up their bod's with oil
Then style and profile all day long
A body's left left to wonderin'
If there's nothin' else they do.

Thank God on this here planet
All people don't look the same
There's another brand of folks
Sportin' a different kind of tan.
The skin is just as bronzed ya know
But the thing that ain't the same
There's only a little bit of hide ya see.

Instead of bronzed from head to toe
The hands and face are all that's tanned.
And when he takes his hat off
A rancher's forehead's white as snow'
Since his clothes are traditional
When a rancher rolls his sleeves to wash
Ya can see his arms ain't tanned at all.

Please let me say in closin'
I don't begrudge them boy's
From workin' on their tans
Just remember there's some around
Whose tan's a little different
But then they're just as proud of theirs
'Cause they got it, workin' on the land

The Sky is Falling

The rollin' prairie lays before my eyes
Expanse of green meets clear blue skies.
Prairies grass waves from a gentle breeze
Grouse and prairie dogs take their ease
In the bosom of the land the Creator made
Coyotes and foxes in the burrows they laid
Their young ones to rest and restore
Each day they hunt the land they explore
To sustain their lives predators must prey
On prairie dogs and grouse they hunt each day.

The cycle of life the Creator has wrought
Has survived man's ignorant onslaught
Had he his way this land would be a car park.
Filled with shoppers, pollution, and several K-Marts.
The earth's been this way how long I can't guess
Mother Earth managed to live through man's duress.
It won't take long before one tiny abscess
Created by man becomes a spreading cancer
Only a few brave souls will have the answer
To save us all from short sighted fools.

Lately I think Mother Earth's plumb mad.
The weather She's making is pretty bad
'Fore ever'thin's gone, we'd best buy a clue
The Creator will make all things brand new
I wonder if man will be in His new plan
Or if He's had enough and deletes the human
Who will care for the earth like He intended
Perhaps man can repair all he's offended
Creator oft' gives more than one chance
Has man reached his limit; is this his last dance?

Is there an answer to man's ultimate fate?
Or in his folly; has he learned much too late?
The wind on the plain is lost in the sky
The wolf's howl on the mountain is amplified
By the cry of the eagle soaring on wings above
They are testament to the Creator's love
This is the beauty that lives in spite of man
They were here before man's history began
These things will live on after man has flown
That Mother Earth can heal is yet to be shown.

Thirty-Five Years Ago

Thirty-five years ago I stood up string straight
My back didn't hurt when I pulled on my boots
My hair wasn't gray and my vision was fine
And some folks said I was downright skinny.

Thirty-five years ago my blood pressure was low
I jogged five miles and pumped iron each day
Why the doc couldn't find no darn cholesterol
Visitin' the bathroom wasn't the highlight of my day

Thirty-five years ago I'd burn the candle at both ends
These days I'd be happy if I could just find the candle
I'd greet each New Year and stay up all night
Now I'm in bed well before the Times Square ball drops

Thirty-five years ago my knees and hips were still made of bone
Today I have more titanium in me than the sky lab in space
I could go through the airport without a backward glance
If I'd try that today, they call me a gal gang terrorist.

Sure alotta things changed in thirty-five years
But there's sure 'nough alotta things I still do . . .
I can still ride my horse anytime I please
I can walk the dogs ever day if I want.

I can count on my friends to visit each day
My family still loves me even when I'm a grouch
I can drive my car any dang place I want
All-in-all I'm pretty healthy for the shape I'm in.

There's lot's a things been the same for 66 years
I can still thank the Creator for all that He's given:
A roof o'er my head and three meals a day
The mountains, rollin' hills, and prairies of home.

He gives me hope for tomorrow and peace of mind
He gives me the freedom to live the life I choose
He helps me laugh when I feel like cryin'
He gives me good neighbors when times are tough.

Thirty-five years ago I had a springier step
My bones didn't creak when of got out of bed
I could sleep on the ground in the mountains at night
I guess you could say I've got no cause to complain

And thirty-five years later I'm still in the game.

I Always Ask Why . . .

Folks who work from dawn to dusk
Workin' the land or maybe a brand
Don't expect to make oodles of dollars
We hope and pray to just break even.

Some years things don't go our way
Maybe the weather don't go right
Cattle or wheat prices take a plunge
Still, we manage to hang on tight.

But 2020 has got to be the worst
Of any year that comes to mind.
A pandemic, political, social mess
The nation's economy went to hell.

All the politicians in Washington
Couldn't get out of each other's way
When citizens needed them most
They were nowhere to be found.

Still, worst of all a nasty election
Divided us right down the middle.
The news depicted violent clashes
Day in day out for most of the year

Vitriol and hatred spewed across the land
Our allies and enemies around the world
Aghast they watched us fuss and fight
And wondered if we'd lost our minds.

On top of that Mother Earth got pissed
And let us know she was still in charge.
The fires and floods and hurricanes
Shook friends and family to their core.

People came out of the woodwork it seemed
To help their neighbors who'd lost the most.
Why can't we act that way day in day out,
Not just when a horrible disaster strikes?

I know good folks must outnumber the bad
There have always been people who hate.
There have always been people who love
Each other without looking for any reward.

I'm looking forward to the day when I won't
Continually have to always ask why . . .

Inventory

Once I knew this crusty ol feller
Who ran a damn big cattle outfit.
Took in all the country here 'bouts
He sure was proud of all he owned.
Had no family 'tween you and me
He spent all his time collectin' more.

One thing sure; he let folks know
His outfit was the best there was.
For miles 'round no one could beat
His hifalutin' bovine masterpiece.
Matter of fact he worked real hard
He made his place stand out by far.

Ever'one agreed his place was fancy.
Hell, there weren't nothin' to compare
With all he'd built over some 50 years.
Critters stood up to their knees in
Broad green pastures and ponds galore.
Heaven above had nothin' to compare.

Now as Clem . . . that was his name . . . aged
He took to wonderin' what he'd do
Since he had no kin to pass all this to
What would become of his palace place
After all the work and struggle to make
His ranch a money making proposition.

Ol Clem sat and pondered his earthly fate
A tear came rolling down his wrinkled face.
He sure 'nough had all a man could want
Riches galore and all kinds of material stuff.
The one thing missin' ol Clem realized was
Family and friends to make life worthwhile.

Folks often wait til it's way too late to
Stop and think 'bout their earthly fate.
They're hell bent for 'lection in a race
To outdo their neighbors just to see
If they can amass riches fit for Midas
The king whose touch turned all to gold.

As for Clem, he died with no one to mourn;
He was laid in a grave so cold and dark.
And Mother Earth has taken Her claim;
Fine green pastures and cool, clear ponds;
No longer have cattle wearing his brand;
Bison and deer have returned to the land.

Clem's is a cautionary tale that's true.
A more pitiful feller yer not likely to see;
He thought he had all a body could want;
His trail ended without family or friends.
Best get yer mind straight lest ya find like
Clem ya never know what matters most.

Movin' On . . .

Folks ain't the same from cradle to grave.
At the worst of times our friends can be vexin'.
When problems 'come too much to handle,
There aint no point in hangin' onto what is gone
More 'n likely it's prob'ly time to be movin' on.

There's worse things than havin' to move.
Just could be a new place is a might excitin'.
Ya meet new folks and have a change of scenery.
The critters ya move have a period of adjustment
But pretty soon they fit in as natural as can be.

Folks change o'r the years til ya just can't get along
Life's pages turned, you can't go back . . . even if ya wanted to.
Bridges get burned, the water flows on, time to be movin' on.
Won't be long and the vexation you felt will be way behind.
Ain't no point in lookin' back for the friendship that you lack.

Daddy once said, "When ya been replaced; don't look so sad,
There's better friends down the road. Just cross 'em off 'cause
They weren't true friends after all. Them's words to live by."
S'pose he's right that's for sure, it's their loss, not mine,
The loss still stings like bees stinging you on the butt.

I don't need their drama just the same, 'cause I got my own.
What's done is done, ain't crying in spilt milk; I'm movin' on.
There's light on the horizon for my ponies and me to be ridin.
Matter of fact one of dad's favorite songs to be singin' . . .

"I'm movin' on . . . I'll soon be gone . . . I'm through with you
Too bad your blue . . . keep movin' on . . ." Hank Snow

The Campfire

At the end of the day cowboys circle up
'Round the campfire eatin' their grub
Ain't too long 'fore the talk gets 'round
To long ago stories of ranchin' and such

One ol boy who's been 'round the block
Tells tales that all cowboys here 'bouts
Swear as sure as the risin' sun in the east
Are true and ain't made up Western lore.

The boys all gathered around were hushed
As a congregation a waitin' the preacher's
Gospel 'bout sin and hell fire and brimstone
What's waitin' for them who break God's law.

Ol Zeke (that was his name) cleared his throat
And commenced his cautionary tale 'bout a poke
Named Hank and his escape from a fiery end
That a storm from hell set the dang prairie alight

Zeke was smokin' his corncob pipe as he talked
The smoke wafted up 'round his face and curled
And mixed with the smoke of the campfire bright
'Fore he spoke he drew a long, long puff his pipe

A new man grew anxious for Zeke to get started
Called in frustration, can't you get on with it, man
Other cowboys 'round the fire were aghast at the
Terrible breach in decorum ol Zeke commanded

But ol Zeke took this lack of edicate in his stride
After all this weren't the first time he'd run into a
Some whippersnapper who thought he knew it all
Grey steely eyes caught the young man's face.

So ya want me to get on with my tale do ya son?
Alright, but afore I commence ya'all must be silent.
Another cowboy knocked the kid upside the head.
Won't be no more interruptions, the cowboy said.

Some time ago, Zeke began, there was a brash
Young cowhand from down Texas way came up
North (to Californios land) who thought no one
Could outdo him at ropin' when tyin' hard and fast.

Them buckaroos said we don't tie hard and fast
What's done round here is dally roping for sure
We use a 60 riata woven from prime rawhide
We swing a big loop to catch the wild bovine.

Not to be out done the young cowboy said if
You want to prove your worth I'm game for
A contest to prove who's the best, in fact I'm
Ready to wager anything agin my best pony

The young cowpoke was leading a really nice
Buckskin gelding sure 'nough big and stout
He was as sound as anything these buckaroos
Had seen; he could hold any snotty ol bovine.

One of the best vaqueros in the land came
Stridin' up and looked the young man's pony
Good over; he said I think I'll just take you up
On your boast; I need a good'un in my string.

All the others standing 'round laughed out loud
'Cause no one could hold a candle to Jaun's
Work with throwing a riata with nary a miss
The man stepped up and shook Jaun's hand.

Ya got a bet and if you lose I'll take yore fancy
Bridle and for sure them silver spurs as well.
With the wager set and the rules spelled out
The buckaroos shook hands and mounted up.

Now between two vaqueros a cranky ol cow
Was laying in the dirt still huffin' and puffin'
A meaner bovine you would never ever see
She was bowin' snot and pulling the riatas

The boss of the crew said turn her loose
And be damn careful of them damn horns
She's yore target and across the rancho
She'll go; the one who brings her back wins.

The young cowboy pulled his hat down tight
He nodded to let her up; she tore the ground
She left vaqueros scattered in the wind; with
Tail in the air she ran as if the devil was chasin'

The cowboys charged off whippin' and spurrin'
They was hell bent to catch greased lightnin'
And around the fire there weren't nary a peep
Punchers were hangin' on every word spoken

Ol Zeke paused to refresh his pipe and took
A long, long puff. The young man was miffed;
Zeke! Get on with it man; what happened next?
Calm yourself you'll get your britches in a bind.

Well to say the least the prairie was in turmoil
The dust was flyin' and cowboys was cussing
Horses were heavin', that bovine was fleeing
When the boys got close, that cow would bolt

Sure looked like neither one of them would win.
Hold up yelled the young man, we ain't gettin'
Nowhere; if that cow's to be caught we'll need
To team up and set a trap for that onery cuss.

Jaun stopped his horse and looked at the boy
What about your bet; as a team you won't win.
The young'un smiled; I think I just did and he
Held out his hand; let's go get that damn devil.

Zeke refilled his pipe, smiled knowingly and
Got up, walked to his bedroll and laid down.
Everyone around the campfire followed suit.
The young man sat there dumbfounded.

Wait, what happened? Who won the bet?
One man turned to him and said no one.
What do you mean, no one. Who was the
Better of the two vaqueros. So who was it.

You'll have to ask Zeke, but I doubt that he'd say
Why, I don't get it; Zeke didn't expect you would.
What happened to the young smart-ass cowboy?
He grew old, wise and tells tales 'round the campfire.

Really, Mom?

We live in the techno age
Sure as hell we turned the page

Our reliance on machines
Has wound up in our genes

Seems we can't go a minute
Machines take hold bit by bit

Social amenities we once knew
Now bein' social has gone askew

No longer do we talk face to face
Conversation has been misplaced

I'll make my point clear as can be
Wasn't too long ago I could see

Techno and horses met full force
Claudia and Dazz are buds of course

But androids and horses don't mesh
Try as she might Dazz couldn't refresh

The rapore she and her friend once
Had but Claudia was being a dunce

By ignoring her friend's subtle plea
She wanted attention that was the key

So Dazz was patient and walked along
Claudia's android was playing a song

When Dazz was at the end of her rope
She picked up some speed into a lope

Dazz turned really sharp and slid to a stop
Claudia nearly ran into Dazz with a wild hop

They stared at each other: one pleading
The other realized they both were needing

A connection not technical but spiritual
Because horses bring out what is lyrical

Dazz's plea was simple as can be
Like really mom can't you see

I want you to pay attention to me
I'm giving to you my time for free

However a catch comes with my brand
I won't play with an android in your hand.

The New Year

Another year has come around
What should I ask as I bow down

Seems to me I pray for the same
Peace, love, respect; I could name

I'd wish all the homeless had a home
A place where they'd be safe and warm

Wretched, grinding poverty would be no more
Prosperity would spread from shore to shore

I'd wish that folks could laying the blame
And just remember from whence we came

The Creator made us like eggs on Easter
You look in the basket color don't matter

When ya take off the shell an egg is an egg
With folks it's the same the difference I beg

Why do some folks look down on others
Seems to me we're sisters and brothers

The year just past has been an almighty trial
For sure everyone has just been plain hostile

I'd wish for a country where all could be
Together as one in an enormous family tree

What if socially, politically, environmentally
We could make a compromise fundamentally

I'd wish this pandemic were under control
And patients in hospitals could all go home

I'd wish first line defenders could get some rest
Ultimately they've given to us their very best

I'd wish businesses could open their doors
And prosperity was once again the norm

I'd wish we could give up the doom and gloom
And recognize folks who are making a difference

No Respect

There was a time not too long ago
Man and nature lived in harmony

The Creator laid out His master plan
With animals and man close at hand

A family with each other prayed
On Mother Earth they did reside

The circle of life went on and on
All life that could be relied upon

For generations we lived this way
But things are different this day and age

Man has destroyed so many things
His lust and greed he needed to assuage

He raped the land and took all he could
Gold and silver, oil and coal, these things he stole

He killed the animals with no remorse
The buffalo and grizzly were on the brink

Coyote and wolves were vermin to die
Even prairie dogs had no place in this world

He built up the cities and tore up the plains
The wild places were on the endangered list

Eagles and peregrines were dying out too
The chemicals and pesticides were doing their job

Mother Earth Herself was terminally ill
The air and water were polluted and foul

Only until man was in danger of dying himself
Did right thinking people get hold of themselves

They cleaned up their mess and the distress was less
But the damage was done, Mother Earth bore the scars

Big business have us all by the throat
The powers that be even dance to their tune

Oil spills and pipelines scar our lands
Still the white man has no respect

When Mother Earth could give no more
The Creator took hold and punished us all

He called Mother Nature to bring down her wrath
Fires and floods have ravaged all in Her path

Winds fanned the flames and destroyed everything
In all Her fury Mother Nature ravaged Mother Earth

The good and the bad have to share this pain
Few were spared from the storm's bloody stain

Those who are left to rebuild and replace
Must remove the scars on Mother Earth's face

In the midst of all this devastation and sorrow
Love and compassion brings hope for tomorrow

People have come together to ease the pain
Of those who have lost without thinking of gain

A shoulder to lean on, an embrace to show care
These simple gestures give strength to repair

No doubt man will rebuild his cities much bigger
They should be careful if they don't figure

Out his is a cautionary tale of the result of greed
When people take more than they need

Without a thought for there is a buffer
When Mother Earth is made to suffer

When we pay no respect to this land
In the end there will be no place to stand

In some future time Creator and Mother Earth
May forgive man's transgressions and move on

But how many chances do you think
They will give us because in a blink

All that we know, if we fail to show
Love and respect for all that is given

When the last bridge has been crossed
And all has been lost; what's the final cost

Ask Mother Earth, only she can foretell
If man has struck his own death knell.

The Quest

I HATE FUNERALS; I hate death. Although inevitable, I will rail against death with all my strength. Of course Grandfather would say that is wasted effort. Even though I was here at the gravesite, my mind was someplace far away. I suppose it's human nature, but I was reliving the events in my grandfather's life, many of them were conflicts between us. I hated that; probably because I had to face myself. A not so pleasant task for most of us. But I was a piece of work . . . I was so bullheaded, immature, hateful, ignorant of our traditions, and just an all 'round pain in the ass for much of my childhood. My grandfather, Joseph Grey Bull, raised me from the time I was two years old. He was a respected elder in our tribe . . . a good man, a wise man, and a very patient man.

DON'T WORRY THEY said . . . you'll be fine they said . . . c'mon, Kid, you're ready for this . . . go get 'em. I'm twenty years old and I'm still The Kid. I really do have a name Marilee (Lee) Grey Bow. I was named for my grandmother. I had no desire to take my father's name, so when I turned eighteen, I legally took my grandfather's sir name.

I have a college degree, Grandfather insisted, but I haven't used it yet. I'm cowboyin' at the Arapahoe Ranch . . . love it. I'm here at the Original Californios Ranch Roping and Stock Horse Contest. This contest features events that mimic the real-life working situations of the buckaroo. The Californios is not a ranch rodeo; the events are not timed. They are judged by a panel of respected judges who study each team and score them. A vaquero is judged on the size of the loop, the distance thrown, the handling of the slack, and the control of the dally. Their horsemanship, handling of the cattle, sportsmanship, and style are all scored and recorded. Cattle are roped out of "the rodear" (herd) as teams of two or three cowboys expertly lay them down for doctoring or branding. Simple, right? This contest is my turn to show the elders I know what I'm doing and will not embarrass my people.

Shorty was right; I am ready for this, but that hasn't always been the case . . .

"Grandfather, what do you mean I can't compete in stock horse roping contests," I complained . . . loudly.

"I'm old enough; I'm just as good a roper as the boys . . . you said so yourself," I continued, "so what is the problem? Go ahead and tell me!"

Grandfather gave me "the look" that sent shivers down my spine. I swear to all that's Holy, he could stare right into your soul with those steely dark eyes.

"Always in the days of my grandfather's, grandfather, and those before them, there was respect from our children for the elders and our traditions. But you show disrespect for our traditions; you forget who you are and your place among our people."

Grandfather wasn't angry. Yet, in his eyes there was great disappointment in a child who obviously would not go quietly back to her "place" among the people.

"Grandfather, you know I have always respected you and our traditions," I countered, "and I don't want to bring scorn down upon our people. I just don't understand why the only reason I can't compete is because I'm a girl."

"Going to these contests is not your place. You can still work with the horses; only if you do your other duties. That is my final word."

There was no point in arguing further. Once Grandfather made up his mind, there was no way he'd change. But I still had one request that was very important to me.

"Grandfather," I asked, "may I still go to work at Mr. Cantrell's saddle shop? I earn money to buy things I need for Dancer."

"Yes, granddaughter. But only after your chores are done."

Grandfather's disappointment aside, I had never been more dejected in my life. Even knowing I was a half- breed bastard child of an Arapaho woman and white cowboy drifter didn't compare with what I was feeling now. My mother had left the rez (Wind River in Wyoming) and went to work at the local tavern, tending bar (and other "stuff") to supplement her income. Trust me, she never spent it on me. Then one day she and my low life drifter father took off. I haven't seen either of them since I was two. I fell into the hands of my mother's parents. They both raised me, that is, until my grandmother died when I was eight. So, my grandfather has had the task of bringing me up in the traditions of my people while withstanding the pressures of the twenty-first century. I know this situation hasn't been easy for him; I think he feels as though he failed with my mother, so he wasn't going to fail with me. He is strict to say the least, but in all fairness, he is even handed with praise and punishment. And most importantly, he does let me work with the horses. He has taught me the traditional way the Arapaho trained horses.

Anyway, I was growing up tough. But still I didn't know where to belong. I was never quite accepted with my mother's people and I sure as hell wasn't accepted with my father's people. Even though my father was a low life good for nothing drunk, he was still on a slightly higher rung in life that a half-breed Arapaho . . . and a girl to boot. There were two places I felt really happy . . . anywhere on the back of Dancer and Wade Cantrell's Saddle Shop.

Wade "Shorty" Cantrell was an old cowboy from way back. He would never tell me just how old he was, he'd only allowed that he was older than dirt. After he became so busted up he couldn't cowboy any longer . . . and he was "danged sure 'nough not gonna build fence," he started mending saddles and tack for the cowboys still employed by the Arapahoe Ranch. In addition, he'd shoe a few horses, anything to stay around the ranch and his friends. The ranch was the only family and home he'd had for the last twenty-five years. Prior to coming to the Arapahoe Ranch, Shorty had cowboyed all over the west . . . Nevada, Montana, Wyoming, and up in the Owyhee country in Oregon and Idaho. At most of these ranches, he did day work; he pretty much stayed on the move. Everything he owned was in his truck and horse trailer and he was happy. He was doing what he wanted, where he wanted. Then, finally, he figured that if he was going to repair tack and such, he might as well get paid for it and opened his own tack shop in Thermopolis, Wyoming. His saddles, bridles, hackamores, and bosals were high demand items. He also made beautiful bits and spurs; he was making a living still close to the cowboy life style he loved.

I don't know why, but he took in a lonely, scruffy, dirty, half-breed kid with an attitude . . . me. He gave me roping lessons and helped me train Dancer in the traditional way the vaqueros trained their bridle horses to be straight up in the bridle. To pay for lessons, I helped him in the shop after school, on weekends, and during the summer. I'd sweep up, run errands, and clerk in the store. We made a good trade . . . the arrangement got me off the rez. I was learning a trade and learning to work horses. What I liked most (when there were no customers) was listening to Shorty's stories. And when an old cowboy came in to pick up some tack or a saddle, their recollections really took off. Sometimes I wondered if some of the things they described really happened or were embellished. Whether true or not didn't matter; I was so engrossed listening to Shorty and his buddies that I completely forgot my crummy life on the rez; until I looked up to see Grandfather enter the shop.

He addressed Shorty with his usual poised and adroit demeanor. He always presented himself as a proud Native, an elder of his tribe; he commanded respect from others, Native or white. The response he received was usually one of respect and admiration, which he'd gained over the years (whenever he dealt with others). He had known Shorty for years; they had worked together on the Arapahoe Ranch. But in this setting—Shorty's shop—he addressed him formally. Which I thought was odd.

"Mr. Cantrell," Grandfather began, "I wish to thank you for allowing my granddaughter to work for you, but it is time for her to come home. She has her own responsibilities that need tending."

"Joseph Grey Bow," Shorty replied, "I am glad to see you. You know you are always welcome here. But ya know, I really am uncomfortable with this formal stuff. I'm Shorty . . . you know that. After all the years we spent working together, I thought we got past this Mr. Cantrell stuff."

Ike Barnes, Shorty's buddy, and the man who had been swapping stories with Shorty, excused himself, rather abruptly.

"Shorty," Ike growled. "I got chores that need tending to. Thanks for repairing this bridle. See ya later."

"Okay, Ike," Shorty answered. "Take care."

There was no way to miss the condescension in Ike's expression. Everyone around knew Ike had no use for Indians. He and General Phillip Sheridan would have gotten on together really well. "The only good Indian is a dead Indian." He really couldn't stand to be in the same room with an Indian. The only reason he tolerated me was because Shorty stood up for me when Ike tried to kick me clear across the room once. Shorty liked to beat him to death. Shorty may be getting old, but he's still a man to stand aside from when he was angry.

"Joseph," Shorty said softly. "Let me apologize for Ike. We've been friends for years. I owe him my life 'cause he's got me out of many a scrape when we was cowboyin' together. I hope ya know I don't go along with his behavior toward you and your people. And he can be a pain in the ass, I know, but what can I say?"

"I understand, Shorty," Grandfather replied. "There are those among my people who are like Ike. We must try to change their outlook toward others not like themselves, but it is hard, very hard."

My grandfather's demeanor suddenly became much more cordial, almost friendly toward Shorty.

"I know, Joseph." Shorty snorted. "Sometimes ya wanna just knock the snot out of 'em, but then again, that doesn't solve anything either. C'mon, let's go out back; we can smoke a pipe or two. I wanna show you that yearlin' colt; he's growin' like a weed. The Kid's been working with him. She might be a short sprout, but she's becomin' a good hand."

Short sprout indeed! Height doesn't matter when you're riding a horse. A good horse was the great equalizer, and at sixteen I didn't feel like a sprout. But he was right . . . I was built pretty close to the ground. And where Shorty's concerned, I don't have a name. He's been calling me Kid for as long as I've known him. I used to keep telling him I had a name, but after a while I just gave up.

"Thank you, Shorty. I would like nothing better. I am glad my granddaughter is learning to work a horse like a Vaquero. In many ways, the Vaquero and the Arapahoe train much the same. It is good for young ones to learn from their elders . . . we have much to offer . . . if they just listen."

I wanted to jump up and down to get their attention. They were talking as though I wasn't even there. So I decided to become a part of the conversation.

"Excuse me," I began, "I am right here. Do you have to talk about me like I wasn't even here? Could I please be part of this discussion?"

The two men stopped in their tracks and turned back to look at me.

"Well I'll be dammed." Shorty chuckled. "The kid's got a voice. Okay, missy, let's hear what ya got to say."

I looked from Shorty to Grandfather. I swallowed audibly. Grandfather had a wry smile at the corners of his mouth.

"Um," I stammered, "it seems to me that since ya can't ride Latigo yet, the right thing to do is ground work. I've been working on getting his trust. I want him to understand that I'm not going to hurt him, but at the same time he needs to follow my commands, we've been getting along pretty good. I have sacked him out, I've taught him to ground tie, and I hobble broke him. I just started round pen training with him. Send him off onto the rail and run him in both directions at the walk, trot, and lope. I want him to turn in to me . . . to face me when I ask him to stop; so far, we've been doing pretty well. Next, I'm going to pony him off Dancer. I want to get him out of the round pen ever now and then to let him see the country. Get him to go through creeks and streams and such."

I stopped and waited for a response from Grandfather and Shorty.

"What do ya think, Joseph?" Shorty asked. "Not too bad for a sixteen-year-old kid, huh? A course, this is all talk. I reserve judgement 'til I see the Kid in action."

Grandfather nodded in agreement.

"What do you say, Shorty?" Grandfather smirked. "Shall we sit down and smoke a pipe while the young one shows us what she has learned?"

"That sounds like a plan," Shorty agreed. "Okay, kid. Joseph and I are going to go sit in the shade while you go to work. So have at 'er."

Horses have always been a huge part of my life; in fact the Arapahoe Nation as a whole relied upon the horse and in general were excellent horsemen (women). At an early age, each Arapahoe child was given a horse to care for. Finally, my turn had come to show these two the lessons I learned as a child stuck. I just hope Latigo would cooperate.

The time has come to pause my tale for a history lesson from the Native perspective, so please bear with me. I often wondered how to explain reservation life to people who have everything, what it's like to live for those who have nothing, who go without basic necessities day in and day out, who are often abused mentally and physically, and eventually deprived of hope as well. Pick a tribe and you will see what Natives endure. Flash back to the 1800s. Understand, not only are the basics of life non-existent, but white Europeans deprived Natives of their culture as well. During the period of westward expansion . . . Manifest Destiny . . . and the resulting Indian Wars, white Europeans completely subjugated Native tribes. Since God was on their side, whites felt justified in demanding Natives assimilate or die. And die we did. If we weren't murdered outright, we were starved, or succumbed to diseases we had no immunity against.

I can't say who suffered more, tribes who were basically farmers or hunter gatherers. For you see, the great tribes of the Great Plains were deprived of the one thing that made them nearly equal, or better than whites . . . the horse. In order to make subjugation complete . . . the Sioux, the Cheyenne, the Comanche, the Nez Perce, and the Arapahoe . . . the buffalo was murdered to the brink of extinction and horses were taken away or killed. That way, in the white man's warped mind, the Indian would never rise again; they would be totally dependent on the white man.

As a precursor to adulthood, young males in Native cultures have to complete a trial . . . some call this trial a vision quest. The young man in question goes out into the wilderness with nothing to help him survive. He has to survive by his own wits. Naturally, after three days without food or water, anyone would have hallucinations, but in Native cultures, these hallucinations are actually visions during which the young male sees his spirit helper. This helper comes from one of these elements: fire, earth, air, or water. Upon his return to the tribe, the young man tells everyone about his quest and is given his adult name. No vision, no transfer to adulthood. The vision quest wasn't just for young males; young adult women also undertook vision quests.

THUS BEGAN MY quest . . .

However, my quest was not going to involve going out into the wilderness to find my spirit helper. I already had mine—the horse. My horse Wapati's Wind Dancer was my rock. He helped me through the tough times when, in my view, he was all I had. When I am with him, the cares of the world fade away. I have been able to train him myself. With the help of Grandfather and Shorty, Dancer has become a first-class cow horse. I was just nine years old when he was foaled. He's seven now and he has become such a part of me, I can't imagine life without him. And now Shorty and Grandfather have given me a chance to train another young horse . . . Shorty's yearling, Latigo.

The two men weren't lying when they said they were going to sit in the shade and watch. There they were, sitting under a tree, smoking Grandfather's pipe. As an aside, I always wondered what it was they were actually smoking. Latigo and I were sweating in this sandy coral. Well, what the heck, I will just work Latigo like always, regardless of the audience. I always let Latigo choose the direction of travel to begin. I liked to free longe him in the beginning, just to get the edge off. Once he had just a slight sheen of sweat, I knew he was ready to listen. The first test . . . will he stop and face me?

"C'mon, buddy," I breathed, "don't make me look stupid."

Just like that, Latigo turned, faced me, licked his lips, and waited. Not bad for a yearling. I put Latigo through his paces. I drove him with long lines, asking him to turn over his hocks in both directions, asked him to stop, and back up. I used the lines to control him at the walk, trot, and lope. The side pull on his head simulates the same pressure as a snaffle bit, but doesn't hurt his mouth. To me, that is most important . . . save a young horse's mouth . . . keep it soft at all costs.

This lesson lasted about twenty minutes and through it all, the men in the shade never said a word. I looked over and shook my head. Dancer was just as noncommittal as the old men. He was saddled up, waiting patiently for his part in the lesson. I lead Latigo over to Dancer, looped the lead around the saddle horn, untied the mecate, and mounted with practiced ease.

"Dancer, Latigo, and I are going for a long walk," I announced. "Do you want to walk along or are you going to sit in the shade all day?"

I'm sure my tone was a little derisive, but I didn't really care. I wanted some feedback, good or bad, but all I got was silence. In my view, that wasn't very helpful. Dang!

Grandfather just gave me "the look," Shorty just nodded.

"Not bad," he said. "At least ya didn't get tangled in them lines and have a big wreck."

Thank you . . . that was helpful, I thought.

I just rode away. Dancer picked up his quick pace with Latigo patiently following alongside. I wasn't out of earshot when I heard Shorty and Grandfather talking.

"My granddaughter shows promise, Shorty. In my opinion, your colt is in good hands."

"Dang straight, Joesph," Shorty hollered. "I am working on a hackamore, bosal, and spade bit for Latigo when the time comes for the kid to use them. And there is something else, Joseph. Ya know I ain't gettin' any younger. I'm not up to riding colts anymore, so I'm going to put Latigo's papers in the kid's name. I'm making him a gift to her."

Grandfather didn't speak at first. Then he smiled.

"Thank you, Shorty. Your generosity is remarkable. To tell the truth, I was going to see about buying Latigo for Lee. She has come a long way with Dancer and Latigo. I truly believe the Creator has touched my grand-daughter and given her a great gift."

How 'bout that! I wonder why they didn't tell me all of this. Maybe they didn't want me to get a swelled head. Oh well, I guess it pays to have good hearing. Still, my dream of competing in ranch roping and stock horse competitions didn't seem to be getting any closer. Hmmm.

Shorty's place wasn't far from the Arapahoe Ranch corrals, and I knew they'd be working cattle today, so I rode over in that direction. I had two choices to get there. The first was very simple; ride down a dirt road, the long way. Second was to go through the prairie, the shortcut. But the shortcut forced us to ride across a bridge, wade through a small stream with water to stirrup height, and cross a bog. Not a problem. Dancer and I had gone this direction many times, but I had never ponied Latigo before. Since Dancer was calm and brave, Latigo should follow him right along. The bridge, no problem, the creek no problem . . . we'd been through water crossings a bunch of times. The bog, on the other hand, was something new. The Arapahoe Ranch hands maintained the bridges and such, but we'd had a pretty good rain a few days before our crossing and the bog was really boggy. The logs across the bog were nearly submerged, but hopefully would support us going across. As I expected, Dancer immediately started across and my prayers were answered when Latigo followed close behind. Crisis averted, we arrived at our destination in record time.

There was the usual controlled chaos at the corrals. As always, the ranch boss had things well in hand; the branding and doctoring was well in progress by the time I arrived. Willie Black Crow was in his late thirties or early forties. He had worked on the Arapahoe since he was my age. Of course he started at the bottom and worked his way up to ranch boss. He was another who took me under his wing and was teaching the art of ranch roping using the long reata. I was getting better with each lesson, so I was hoping he might let me try my hand at dragging a calf or two to the fire. I didn't say anything, I just waited. Patience is a virtue Grandfather would say, a virtue I was slow to grasp. Still, it didn't take long before Willie noticed me.

"Watcha just doing sittin' there," Willie called. "Tie up that colt and get in here. We're a little short-handed and we could use a good roper."

I looked around, a little puzzled; they weren't short-handed. That was just Willie's excuse to get me in on the work. I sure wasn't gonna give him time to change his mind. Quickly, I tied up Latigo, making sure he was tied securely and out of the way. In short order, I was inside the corral with my loop built ready to go.

"Lee," Willie shouted. "Get that little black baldy over there in the corner."

Great, I'd have to wade through the herd, avoid a cranky mother, and make a corner shot without very much room to work.

"Gotcha, Willie," I called. Oh well, in for a penny, in for a pound.

I tried to remember everything all my mentors had been trying to teach me. Everything seemed to be running together. Fortunately, Dancer put me exactly in the right place. I threw my loop, set the trap, and pulled my slack. The whole procedure seemed to take forever, but in actuality, only a few seconds. Success! I had my calf and headed for the fire. The branding crew did their job quickly and efficiently; they set the calf free and I rebuilt my loop to be ready for another throw. Willie didn't say a word. As a matter of fact, you would think he never acknowledged my work, but you can bet he knew exactly what was going on . . . what everyone was doing.

I spent the day dragging calves to the fire. I was having the time of my life . . . Latigo, not so much. He was getting bored standing tied for so long, but on the other hand, he was learning patience. That's ironic isn't it. Me trying to teach patience. Still, I knew I shouldn't press my luck, so I rode over to Willie to let him know I had to go.

"Willie," I said, "I probably better get Latigo back, don't you think?"

"Yeah," Willie replied. "He's been pretty good, but short lessons work the best. I'll see you back at Shorty's one of these days."

I turned to go get Latigo. The look on his face said, "c'mon mom I wanna go home." I took a dally around the horn and got my colt all lined out when Willie walked over.

"Hey, Lee," Willie said. "You did pretty good today, pretty handy. By the way, if your grandfather will let you, we have ranch ropin' practice Wednesday evenings at my place. Why don'tcha come over? Maybe we could give you a few pointers about reata ropin'."

"Hot dang," I exclaimed, "I'd love to. I think Grandfather would let me; if I get my chores and homework done."

"Ya know," Willie said. "You could always have Joseph come along. He was a pretty fair roper himself, back in the day, and it would be a sign of respect to invite him. That would probably make it easier for you to get his permission. You know, make him feel like he is part of your life . . . other than just an authority figure."

I'll be danged. All this time, I had never taken my grandfather's feelings into consideration. He was always there; just as constant as night and day. I had been unfair and misguided.

"Yeah, I never thought about that before, Willie. You're right. I guess that's kinda unfair not putting myself in Grandfather's place. It isn't easy for him to raise a sixteen-year-old kid, huh?"

"That's right, Lee. Especially someone who is as hard headed as you." Willie laughed.

"Thanks a bunch, Willie," I joked. "But you're probably right. I'll see you Wednesday, I hope."

The ride home was uneventful and I had some time to think about Willie's advice about my relationship with Grandfather. Maybe I should take to heart the old saw that says, "you can catch more flies with honey than vinegar." I could be a little more respectful and less argumentative with Grandfather. I just get so frustrated when Grandfather doesn't listen. Then I get angry and just like that the fight's on. Could it be that the reason Grandfather doesn't "seem" to listen has to do with my crummy attitude? Now that I think about it, I'm willing to bet he hears everything, but doesn't respond because of my disrespect. Well, I'll be dipped.

There was a note at Shorty's place telling me to take Latigo home with me. "Hey kid, it would be easier for you to work

Latigo if he was at your place. I'll be checking in from time to time." Wow, that is a surprise. Shorty must have more faith in me than I thought. I was unsaddling and grooming the horses when Grandfather came into the barn.

"You are later than usual, Lee," Grandfather said. "I imagine you must have forgotten you have chores here that must be done as well."

Instead of getting defensive, I simply nodded.

"Yes, Grandfather," I said quietly. "I was at the Arapahoe Ranch corrals; I guess that isn't a very good excuse for being late, but I'm still in time for evening chores. I'll finish putting the horses up, then I'll get to work. I was helping Willie work cattle. He let me drag calves to the fire."

I was beginning to get excited. I was pretty proud of myself. And suddenly it occurred to me this was the opening I needed to convince Grandfather to come with me to roping practice on Wednesday. Chores first, I thought.

"It won't take long for me to do the chores, Grandfather. Then I will come in and fix our dinner."

My sudden excitement didn't go unnoticed. As Grandfather left, I thought I saw the corners of his mouth turn up, just slightly, but a smile is a smile is a smile.

I fixed Grandfather's favorite meal, which didn't go unnoticed either. After all, what did I have to lose? Someone said the quickest way to a man's heart is through his stomach. While we were eating, I broached the subject of roping. First, I asked about Grandfather's day.

"Grandfather, after we finished at Shorty's place, what else did you do with your day," I asked, knowing full well he spent every Monday with the tribal elders.

"The elders spent most of the afternoon arguing about what to do with that dry patch of ground north of the old mission," Grandfather grumbled. "I don't know why they bother. There is no water and the cost of digging a well there is too much. I don't think we'd use the land enough to bother. I would have had more fun if I had gone to the corrals with you."

Holy crap! This is just the opening I needed. This was better than I could have ever hoped.

"Grandfather," I ventured. "I would like to spend more time with you like we used to. Remember when we used to go fishing together. You know, things like that."

"Are you asking to go fishing, Granddaughter." Grandfather smiled.

"Well not exactly," I replied. "Um, this is something a little different, but something we could do together. Willie asked if we would like to come to ranch roping practice on Wednesday evenings. He said they practice every week at his place. I didn't know this, but he said you were a good roper back in the day. I would really like to rope with you."

I tried to sound sincere because I knew he could see right through me trying to butter him up.

"Oh he did, did he!" Grandfather laughed. "Well, that is the truth. Shorty and I worked together for a long time before Shorty was injured. When Shorty came to the Arapahoe Ranch, I was the ranch foreman."

My jaw must have hit the dinner table.

"Yes, Lee," Grandfather continued. "I was the ranch foreman. This was when your mother was your age. I grew up working the land the Creator gave us. When the whites came to this land, we were given a land allotment much smaller than when my grandfather's grandfather lived. So rather than be dependent on handouts from the white man, our people put all our money together to buy cattle. That was the beginning of the Arapahoe Ranch. As we became more successful, we bought more land and expanded out herds. I haven't roped in years. Still . . ."

I had no idea about Grandfather's early life. Of course I knew he and Shorty worked together. But I really never made an effort to learn much about Grandfather's life or my people's traditions for that matter. Maybe the time has come for me to pull my head out of my you know what and grow up.

"Grandfather," I asked. "Does this mean we could go rope together on Wednesdays? I would be proud to be your partner."

There, a first step. A small step to be sure, but maybe from now on we would both be willing to bend and just maybe Grandfather would let me enter ranch ropings. Heck maybe we could even be partners.

"Granddaughter," my grandfather said softly, "I would be proud to rope with you has well."

A beginning had indeed been made. Grandfather and I roped together every Wednesday. Even Shorty came over from time to time to watch, although it was bittersweet for Shorty because he could no longer participate. But he came and cheered us on anyway. I must say we had the time of our lives. In fact we so looked forward to our Wednesday evenings together, Grandfather even did my chores when I was in school so we could leave sooner. We even instigated a new tradition . . . on the last Wednesday of every month we had a pot luck dinner and all the roper's families came. These days became a bonding time for Grandfather and me. Who would have thought horses, cows, and a length of rawhide rope could have drawn us so close together?

So that is pretty much how the next couple of years went. I continued to work for Shorty after school and on weekends. I worked with both Dancer and Latigo every day and watched over Grandfather, who's health began to fail. With all of that, I still managed to keep my grades up and graduated from high school a year early. That was grandfather's proudest moment, not just the fact that I graduated, but also because I got to give the valedictorian speech. Finally, standing on the stage giving my speech, I understood why Grandfather fought so hard to get me into the public school in Thermopolis instead of the reservation school. He knew I would get a better education, sad but true. He realized making sure I got a good education was the best thing he could ever do for me. Shorty was so proud he was about to bust and could hardly wait for the ceremonies to be over so he could give me my graduation present. I was so surprised and grateful I was speechless . . . he presented me with Latigo's papers transferred into my name. I just broke down in tears; I was so happy.

Fortunately, my grades were good enough to get me into the University of Wyoming in Laramie. I thought I'd get a degree in equine reproduction, then I could get work in equestrian facilities, or even a university someplace. What I really wanted to do was come back home and go to work on the Arapahoe Ranch, but Grandfather wanted me to set my sights higher, although I couldn't see anything higher than working cattle on our people's ranch.

But rather than disappointing my grandfather, I worked hard, got my degree—in three years, thank you very much—and got a job managing the horse operation at a fancy ranch outside Laramie. At twenty years old, I was ready to kill bears with a stick. Sadly, that job lasted only six months. Seems some of the clients objected to an Indian running the show, so I left and came back home. By this time, Grandfather was not able to care for himself; I thought it was about time I took care of him. Willie was still the ranch manager at the Arapahoe Ranch, so he gave me a job. I took on the task of overseeing the ranch's horse breeding operation—my fancy college education at work. I was happy, my grandfather was proud, and Willie no longer had to worry about whether or not the breeding operation was in good hands. This was a win-win-win proposition. YAY!

This brings me back to where I started. Willie and I were about to take our turn roping. My job was to go into the herd—rodear—and bring out a calf, drag him to the fire, and let Willie do his thing. Without going into great detail, suffice to say, we did well on that day. I handled my nerves and did my job . . . I just kept telling myself this wasn't any different than working cattle in the home ranch corrals. The most important thing was that I didn't disappoint my grandfather and my people who were in attendance, *en masse*. I finally made Grandfather proud. YAHOO BUCKAROO!!

I SUPPOSE, IN retrospect, my life has come full circle. My grandfather always told me the Creator has a plan for us all. We have a place in the universe, we are a part of Mother Earth, and She is a part of us. The Earth is in the form of a circle; it represents our lives which follow the turning of the earth. Everything in our environment is cyclical: the seasons—spring, summer, fall, and winter—follow one after the other. Each season represents a segment in our lives: childhood, adolescence, adulthood, and respected elder, for lack of a better term. More importantly, each of us never really end. Our spirits, the essence of who we are continues on. This is our destiny and no matter how hard we try, we can't run away from that.

The last thing Grandfather said to me was just a few hours before the Creator called him home. He spoke to me in our Native language . . .

Neisie,

Ceh'e3hi. Kookoh'eeneb3en. Nonoo3e3en. Too3iho netesih' e. Hoonowu3ecoonoo. Hii3oobee' noh ceebe' eico' ouute neyey' eenei3oobei.Toyou'uuwu heethetiine' (i) tiitoonin.

Nii' i3ecoonoo. Neniiceenohoo3e3en. Heetnootowuune3en nehe neenihiibie'3eit woxhox.

Ciibehciini' i3ecoo. Kookoh' u3ecoonoo hoowounouhunoo. Hiinono' eininoo. Heetihniini'cowo'oon.

Biixoo3e3en.

Grandchild,

Listen to me. I am thinking of you. I am leaving you, I am following my wife. I have happy thoughts. It is right and important above all to be honest. You had better remember our traditional way of life.

I am glad. I am giving you a gift. I will leave you this Appaloosa horse.

Don't feel bad. I am thinking I am lucky. I am an Arapahoe. Farewell. I love you.

Perhaps, in the end, that was the most important lesson of all.

T.K. Galarneau was born and raised in North Central Idaho in a small farming and ranching community called Nezperce where she graduated in 1969. She received a BS degree in English and History from Lewis-Clark State College in Lewiston in 1973. Terrie taught American Literature and History in several schools including the Nez Perce Reservation in Lapwai, Idaho before moving to California in 2001 to continue her teaching career. Terrie is also one-eighth Blackfoot. Since she retired from teaching, she enjoys researching Native culture. She now makes her home in the Bay Area with one dog, four cats, and two horses. When she's not teaching or writing, she spends most of her time riding.

Visit T.K.'s website: https://bunkhouseramblin.weebly.com

www.ingramcontent.com/pod-product-compliance
Lightning Source LLC
LaVergne TN
LVHW090129160826
845673LV00015B/1180

9781960373281